AF433846

CONTENTS

The Book of SPIFE... *SPIFE* up *your life!*

MY DESIRE

Everything that is expressed within everything that I have written and will write comes from my personal life experiences. All my opinions, thoughts, philosophies, and ideas are a combination of my accumulated life experiences that I have chosen to share with the world. They are mine alone. I am not a doctor of any sort. I don't, nor will I ever claim to have the answers to any of life's endless questions. I am sharing my observations of the things that have taken place in my life and how those things affected me and my life. Those things have shaped who I am and will continue to sculpt and refine me as long as I am willing to let them. My ONLY (all caps, bolded, and italicized) desire is to help someone... anyone gain some sort of understanding of what this journey or quest called life is really about. At the least, to appreciate and enjoy life for what it is and has to offer. I am certain

I will be criticized and judged for my thoughts and expressions. However, I have long realized that everyone can't agree on everything or see everything the same way. Therefore, I embrace the criticism, judgment, and other perspectives for they will provide more content for me to consider, learn and grow from.

THE COMPLETE BEING

We - human beings - are quite complex creatures, comprised of multiple departments, compartments, thoughts, and emotions that are the embodiment of each individual's personality. Many books have been written on that very subject (human beings) alone. We have studied ourselves since the beginning of our very existence and will continue to do so until our eventual end. This is my modest attempt to contribute to the study. As I study myself and others I realize that we are made up of distinct states of being that when combined are greater than the sum total of each state. This will be an exploration of the complete or whole state of being.

TRANSFORMATION

Change…

As you travel through life - taking what life gives you and going where life leads you - your life is a journey. The journey ends when you decide to take charge of your life and to live it on your terms… your life becomes a quest!

Change is seldom easy. It requires sacrifice and courage. You must sacrifice your old and have the courage to become someone you have never seen but perhaps only imagined before…

"The pain of change can be immense when you are both the sculptor and the sculpture." (Author unknown)

"The Hammer Strikes"

They walked together hand in hand, companions on a journey. For many, many years they followed the path that was laid before them in complete agreement and on one accord. Mind and Figure saw eye to eye. They were loved, one to the other. They were content. Then, there came an uneasiness between them. Mind saw something that changed everything... a vision. Mind became restless. The vision was beautiful and soon became an obsession of Mind and it began to yearn for its realization. Figure had no understanding of visions; it knew only of safety and comfort... it knew only of contentment. Mind changed. It no longer saw contentment but, only its vision. It began to make plans. Figure became concerned when Mind decided to leave the journey's path and set out to create its own path... its quest for its vision. Figure thought, "Surely Mind is lost and needs guidance back to the

the journey's path of contentment." "What shall we do on this quest and how shall we survive?" Figure asked Mind. "We seek freedom, and we will prosper." answered Mind. "Are we not already prosperous?" Figure asked and then continued. "We are safe and content on a path that we know. The only freedom from that is death. I fear that is the only freedom your vision has reserved for us!" Figure shouted with great protest. "I fear that we are already dying, slowly with each and every step of our predestined journey." Mind quietly replied. With great disdain, "Where or how did you acquire this false vision?" Figure asked. "It has been with us for many years, but you have always refused to acknowledge its very existence." answered Mind. Overwhelmed with fear, Figure screamed, "I refuse to acknowledge it still and I refuse to move!" "We cannot travel this life, one without the other." pleaded Mind.

"This I know… and I refuse to move." replied Figure. "You must have courage, trust, and belief!" Begged Mind. "I trust our old path and believe your new path leads to destruction! I wish to live; therefore, I shall not move. You are the one who changed, and I will never change. I refuse!" Insisted Figure. Fear and doubt now consume Figure. Sorrow overtakes Mind for what is to come. There is much pain at the crossroads: stay on the current path or create a new path. The tears begin to flow as Mind is made up and decides…

Change is imminent.

The goal is clear and must be achieved. This existing figure is not fit for the quest. The goal must be achieved... change is imminent. Mind has a vision this Figure cannot realize.

The hammer and chisel: lovers of change are sought. They have reshaped history, redirected destiny, and forged new paths for hundreds of years and will continue to do so for many years to come.

Figure refuses to attune. *The change will commence. The chisel is raised and poised for precise impact. The hammer is provoked... then... it strikes! The timeless lovers collide with extreme pain and desire. The passion of their meaning has begun. Mind wails in agony, Figure shudders as fear erupts. The lovers dance... it strikes! The pain is intolerable; it must be suffered. It strikes! The vision is clear and must be realized. It strikes! Unworthy fragments disperse with every blow... it strikes! "Why so much* pain?!" *Figure begs. It strikes! "I ask the same!" Mind replies. It strikes! Figure cries out; its undesired fleeting and fleeing. Mind morns their departure. It strikes! "Are we not loved?!" Figure pleads. It strikes! "Yes... yes, we are loved!" Mind assures. It strikes! Shrouded in doubt, "Why then? Why do you torture?" Figure insists. It strikes! "For we are loved!" Mind exclaims. It strikes! "We are loved!" Mind repeats. It strikes! The pain becomes excruciating. "This dance must end, for if it continues much longer, you shall be lost!" Figure attempts, desperate to remain. It strikes! "How long must we endure their dance upon us?" Figure asks. It strikes! "Their dance ends when our eyes meet, and our vision shared" Mind explains. It strikes!*

So much agony, for such a task; they lament...

Over time, the lovers rest. Old bits and pieces lie scattered about in the wake of their dance. Mind and Figure sit, exhausted. "Where is my old? I am not recognized." Figure states and then continues with tears streaming down, "You held the lovers at task for so long!" Mind gently brushes away the remaining loose debris and with a kind breath, blows away the fine dust. With a loving smile, "We are… new." Mind says tenderly. Still trembling, Figure looks into the eyes of Mind, "I am?" Figure timidly asks. "We have been changed; sculpted and made ready for our quest." Mind softly explains. Then, after a closer, more intent look, Figure is overcome with a joyous realization and shouts, "I am recognized… WE are… new!" They embrace. "Our eyes have met, for the dance has ended and the lovers rest!" Figure exclaims. Relieved and with overwhelming happiness, they praise, "The pain and agony are no more!" With their tears, together, Mind and Figure wash away any remaining memories of old. They heal the wounds of their ordeal and celebrate it. With tremendous gratitude, they kiss the lovers and bid them farewell. No more fear, no more doubt. Hand in hand they set out on their quest. With courage and belief, they proclaim in complete agreeance and on one accord, "Our vision is clear... now, let us realize it!"

Change was necessary.

Tri

FROM JOURNEY TO QUEST

I journeyed through life with no direction or purpose. I lived my life according to what life sent my way. I took what life gave me and floated around as a wondering leaf who went wherever the winds of life blew me. I did have choices and made my own decisions, but they were merely reactions to what came my way. I never really took charge of my life. I was a passenger on a journey called "my life."

Then the awakening happened... I found my purpose! I no longer wanted to just go with the flow of what life sent my way. I wanted to take charge and control of my life...

This story is not new. This same story has been told time and time again, over and over throughout time. I can confidently say that it will continue to be told in the times to come. The difference, however, is that it was told by individuals with their own, unique perspectives and circumstances. My story is just that, told from my unique point of view. The object being simultaneously viewed of course is called "life". To me, life is like a vehicle that is powered by the wind. We ride in the vehicle and travel wherever the wind carries us. We feel like we are driving... like we are in control. But if that is the case, if we are truly in control... why do we always end up somewhere we don't want to be? We were never in control; we were merely reacting to what the wind blew our way or blew us into.

My experiences with life led me to the same crossroads as many others. It was time to make a choice. Do I continue on the same road, traveling as a passenger along for the ride, with no control over where I end up? Or, should I move into the driver's seat, get off the road completely and create my own, new pathway in the direction of my choosing?

That was the day that my journey ended, and my quest began. I stopped wondering what would happen next and started planning what would happen next. I saw my goal and created a plan to reach it. I took control of my life! I was no longer a passenger on the journey. I became the driver of my quest. When you are on a journey, you are the passenger, just along for the ride. When you are on a quest, you are the driver... so... I'm going for a drive!

It all began early one morning as I lay in my Las Vegas resort hotel bed. It was about three o'clock in the morning when I awoke to many exciting thoughts about the possibilities of my future life. I was in Vegas for an event that was to aid me in achieving my new, better life. When I first joined the company that produced the event, I had recently split up with my wife (a second time) and was searching for ways to make more money and be able to work from home. I also just needed a change. It was through this company that I was shown many different ways to make money online. I learned about e-commerce stores, creating funnels, email marketing, and the power of social media as a tremendous platform for advertisement. I experienced the wonders of a great seminar and how it can touch and positively motivate people. I was also introduced to several books that I hadn't read, by authors I hadn't heard of. I never was a big reader so; I got the audio versions of most of the books. I read some too.

I thought the books would be entirely about how to make money, but then I found they were so much more. They spoke about change within me and what type of person I would need to become to acquire the money that I wanted. Things I never knew or contemplated. Things that opened my eyes to the greater possibilities that have always existed, but I just couldn't see.

So, I paid more money to attend the event that the company put on twice a year. The event was awesome, by the way, and I would definitely do it again. After the first day of the event, I awoke in my bed early the next morning to my mind racing with so many positive thoughts and ideas. That is when it all came to me. I foresaw an objective that I wanted to accomplish... a mission. I also saw my mission become something even greater. It became a vision! Now, this wasn't some divine anointing of heavenly wisdom, instead, it was some great ideas I could see clearly which ignited passion within me. A lot of it was derived from the books I read and listened to, along with things I had experienced throughout my life. For the first time in my life, I recognized my purpose.

My transition from my life's journey to my life's quest took place at that very moment. Of, course I didn't realize at the time that I had transitioned, but I did know I had a purpose! I always had some sort of goal in my life, but no purpose. Get a job, get a better job. Get a girlfriend, get a better girlfriend. Get a better car. Make more money. So on and so forth. I was in the midst of trying to make more money when I discovered my purpose.

It was then that I realized that the company I had joined to help me make more money, was really for someone who already had money or the means to get more. It was not for someone who didn't have much money.

That is when my mission began to form. I wanted to help people with little to no money get out of their situations and become the person they wanted to be and make the money they wanted to make. I wanted people to be able to create a better life for themselves. The only problem with that idea was that I wasn't much better off myself. But it didn't matter. I saw the mission and it needed to be accomplished.

My mission became my purpose. I also had a vision that goes well beyond my mission, but I will talk about that another time after I accomplish my mission. Because of my purpose, the change took place. My journey through life in the passenger's seat, floating along to wherever life took me had ended. I began my quest, with me in the driver's seat, in control of my future.

PART 1: **SPIFE** GUIDE

CHAPTER 1: **INCEPTION**

When I was young -like most children- I was very carefree. I was a typical boy, always getting into things and doing things I knew I shouldn't. This got me into lots of trouble, very often. My father was a stern yet fair man who wanted me to grow up to be a productive and responsible man (like he was). Because of this, he had a low tolerance for my nonsense and downright hardheadedness. He was always swift to punish with a "nip it in the bud" attitude. Eventually, I gained some understanding of what was expected of me and decided to pay more attention to my ways. From that point forth I began to study myself. I learned about myself at an early age. I knew my likes and dislikes, my strengths and weaknesses. I had a young, developing sense of personal growth and self-improvement that matured over the years as life's lessons and challenges came and went.

The second breakup between my wife of twenty years and me was (to say the least) a "tremendous challenge". When you are connected to someone for so long, it is very difficult to sever that connection in a short period of time. Our marriage wasn't horrible. We had problems that needed to be addressed, but I guess we were too tired to work on fixing them. We both simply said, "I'm not happy" and that was the entire summation of our twenty years together. I have to admit our split was probably necessary for us to maintain any type of positive relationship in the future. After all, we still have kids and a business that we run together. We both agreed that it is much better to get along.

The aftermath was where the lessons and challenges began. First things first... I had to get back to me, myself, and I. I had to get back to Tri. I found myself living alone again at the age of fifty-two. My emotions were all over the place. I was happy without her and sad at the same time. I praised the dawning of my new life as I mourned the dusk of my old life. I wanted a mental and emotional change of scenery. I desired something new in my life. I decided that I needed to make more money and I wanted to do it from home. As I mentioned earlier, I found what appeared to fit my plan perfectly, "make money online, anywhere around the world". This was the very first step toward my purpose. I failed to mention that I ended up spending way more money than I made, and the company eventually folded. Nevertheless, my purpose was discovered.

After discovering my purpose, my desire to pursue and live it began to blossom. I could see it clearly and completely and I wanted it with compelling passion. I realized to live within my purpose, I would have to take on a new approach to my life. My purpose must become my life.

The old me was not capable of living this purpose nor equipped to pursue it. I needed to change who I was to become the person who could attain this purpose. I knew what needed to be changed and what could or had to be done to make the changes. I would need to develop a mindset of perseverance and determination. I needed to become less distracted and more persistently focused. I knew I needed to make more money and live healthier. I had to gain a better understanding of who I am. I had to learn that our emotions make us who we are and, at the same time, can and (at times) must be kept under our control. I had to learn to accept my feelings and the things I could not control and create ways to deal with them positively. I had to gain more knowledge about what could help me attain my purpose. I really wanted to improve my life in all aspects to make my quest towards my purpose more easily attainable.

In my quest to attain my purpose, I became more in tune with myself and noticed how certain things would affect my mood or state of being. I observed how feeling happy made it easier to work out and how working out made me feel happy. I found that after meditating, my anxiety and stress levels dropped, and it was easier to focus on resolving the thing that was causing the anxiety and stress in the first place. Of course, getting some extra cash always made everything better... an unexpected expense, not so much. I noticed my different states as they were affected in different situations and how the effects influenced my other states. I learned that by improving one state I could indirectly improve another. I started eating better and dedicated myself to a scheduled workout routine. I started reading books on self-improvement and personal growth. I practiced meditation and communed with nature every chance I got. I read books on finance and ways to make my money work for me.

My plan came to life and slowly began to take shape. I was doing all the right things, but something was off. My actions lacked continuity. I realized this when a problem would arise, I would react differently to each problem depending on my state of being and which individual state was being affected. For instance, if I caught a cold I would focus on my physical state. When a money issue arose, I would focus on my financial state.

However, I also noticed the better I felt with each individual state combined, the easier it was to solve the problem. I began to focus on that observation... all of my states working together as a whole. I developed ways to make each state better through different types of practices and exercises. I kept each state level as high as I could and let them work together as one complete or whole state of being. I found this made dealing with the issues much easier. The more I applied this practice the better my life became. Then I realized, that by focusing on my whole state of being, I was actually focusing on myself as opposed to my problems. No wonder my life felt better!

Hence, the concept of SPIFE was born...

CHAPTER 2: **SPIFE**

Our whole state of being consists of five distinct, yet intricately connected states of being: Spiritual, Physical, Intellectual, Financial, and Emotional... our S.P.I.F.E. Okay, I won't lie, I cheated and changed "Mental" state to "Intellectual" state. I had to arrange the letters in some way to create an acronym that resembled some semblance of a word. Just imagine the other arrangement possibilities. "S.P.I.F.E." is clearly the best choice. That works out also because SPIFE rhymes with life and you will soon realize that SPIFE is life!

The separation of states of being is not a new concept and has been recognized for many years. However, the inclusion of the "financial" state of being is rare. Most would argue that one cannot possess a financial state of being, but as I have observed and continue to observe, it becomes clear that one does possess this state whether acknowledged or not. Our financial state can also be recognized as our ability to interact with others through some form of trade or compromise. Human beings have always possessed this state well before the invention of money. The greater our ability to interact well with other human beings in this manner, the greater our chance for a successful life. Our financial state has always played a vital role in our very survival; long ago and still today. If you consider each state and the effects they have on an individual and the individuals they are associated with, it becomes more evident that the financial state of being is just as impactful as the other more accepted states. I have chosen to add it because of the overwhelming facts that support this idea. For example, how is your day when you are (S) disconnected,

(P) tired, (I) forgetful, (F) broke, and (E) sad? Conversely, when you are (S) in-tuned, (P) spunky, (I) sharp, (F) loaded (not drunk), and (E) happy. Now Imagine both scenarios and the effects they would have on you and those around you. Your financial state plays an equally important part in both examples.

These individual states are a synergic relationship that when combined creates the whole or complete being. Dictionary.com defines synergy as: "the interaction of elements that when combined produce a total effect that is greater than the sum of the individual elements, contributions, etc.; synergism". This synergism is the essence of SPIFE.

SPIFE requires balance or more precisely, is balance. Let's imagine a scale from one to ten, one being "low" and ten being "high" (zero means you are dead, for perspective's sake). The goal, of course, is to raise each state to the highest level possible and keep it there for as long as possible. I call it "SPIFE optimization".

What do you do when you plan a driving trip to a somewhat distant place? Before you begin your travels, you would check the air pressure of the tires on your vehicle. You would check the gas, oil, water, brake fluid, transmission fluid, and whatever else I have missed. You would make sure all these items are at their optimal levels. If the trip is long enough, you would do periodic checks of these levels and would make the necessary adjustments to keep each level optimized as you make your way towards your destination. Knowing you have done so will give you a sense of peace and greater confidence that you will reach your destination the way you planned. Most of us are on a quest of some form or other, with our eyes set on a desired destination. Having optimized states of being will help make our travels much more peaceful and our destinations feel more easily attainable.

Many things affect each state in numerous ways. The practice is to be able to make the necessary adjustments to optimize each state when needed, each day. This brings up the question, "How is your SPIFE today?" The goal of this guide is to help individuals learn how to adjust each of their states of being to achieve the highest SPIFE setting possible, daily. Let's say your day has started great and things are going along fine when suddenly - out of the blue - something arises that causes a momentary disruption to your great start. Through your SPIFE, an on-the-spot adjustment may be needed and can be made to put you back on track.

CHAPTER 3: **KNOW YOURSELF**

I need to make one slight, but especially important digression. As I am writing this, ideas and thoughts tend to surface in my mind and can sometimes interfere with the flow of the writing. That's not a bad thing. It just creates a pause where I stop and make notes before the thoughts get lost. Before I return to writing, I read through some of what I have already written to regain my thoughts and writing flow. As I was reading, I noticed I missed one crucial point. Here it is: The most important factor in this entire concept - even perhaps in just living your life - is to know yourself! Before any form of personal growth or self-improvement can take place, you must know yourself.

You need to know your strengths and weaknesses, your likes and dislikes... your fears. What do you want to change? What do you need to to change? Why do you want or need to change? There are so many questions you should already have the answers to.

How does one go about learning themselves? If you are not sure, take the time to find out. Study and observe yourself. Get to know who you are. There are many things, situations, and challenges that can help define who you are. Unfortunately, pain can serve as a great teacher. The loss of a loved one or the breakup of a long relationship are some examples. I once heard someone say, "If it hurts, you can learn from it." How you react or respond to the problems and challenges can prove to be a true indicator of who you are.

We are constantly bombarded with things that test who we are, which presents opportunities for us to learn more about ourselves. Being mindful or aware of these events and how we respond to them gives us the chance to become more intimate with who we are.

Once you can truly be honest with yourself about yourself, then growth and change can begin. This is important to SPIFE because knowing yourself will allow for an accurate assessment of your state levels and better means of making the necessary adjustments for SPIFE optimization.

SPIFE makes up the complete person and when each state is optimized, the more complete that person is. SPIFE is life. Just think about that for a moment. Think about how each separate state affects you and any combination essentially controls your life. Your SPIFE directly affects the decisions you make every time you make them. SPIFE can also function as a filter for your life. It can be a way to help you assess, consider and deny the things that are detrimental to you, and assess, consider and allow the things that are beneficial to you.

Now, before I continue, I have to clarify something. SPIFE is not intended for us to over-think everything in every situation or circumstance. However, when you first begin to practice the use of SPIFE in your life, it is important to be thorough. Conscious thought and effort must be used. Become more aware of your choices and decisions and what you do to improve your states. It takes time and persistent practice to eventually create a natural SPIFE response to any given exigency.

The most important thing to note is that SPIFE is personal; it is uniquely yours. Your mood, your responses, your personal life situations, and circumstances are all affected and influenced by your SPIFE. Therefore, there is no "one way" to enhance or optimize your SPIFE. What works for you may not work for someone else. What makes one person stronger may not affect another. This reinforces the importance of knowing yourself. For instance, to raise your spiritual state of being you might pray, go for a hike, meditate, go to church, observe the stars or read a book. Whatever your spiritual belief may be, optimize your spiritual state through whatever practice applies to your belief. The philosophy of SPIFE is to be as complete as possible by focusing on your five states of being as opposed to focusing on your problems and the negative things that come your way each day. By recognizing that each state holds equal value for your entire being, you begin to build a stronger, more complete you with the tools to manage daily issues and to view those issues differently.

Each state affects the other positively or negatively. When you have a cold, how does that affect your other states? What if you get a big bonus from work? When you are feeling down emotionally, how do you use your SPIFE to help you feel better? (I) You can call a friend or loved one. (I) You might read a book or watch an uplifting movie. In addition, you can raise your spiritual state by meditating and raise your physical state by going for a walk. These actions will effectively lift your emotional state. That's the synergism I mentioned earlier. Of course, I am not ignoring the fact that in some situations, professional help may be required. If that is the case, please do not hesitate to get the help you need! I will discuss all the various methods of SPIFE optimization in more detail in the later chapters.

The core of SPIFE is all about getting to know yourself by recognizing and understanding your different states of being. By focusing on your

SPIFE... you begin to focus on yourself. SPIFE is who you are. The better you know yourself, the easier it is to optimize each state and raise your overall SPIFE. The greater your SPIFE, the greater your ability to take on whatever comes your way. It changes how you view everything in life. Problems become challenges and challenges become growth opportunities. Not only do you end up in a positive state of mind but also, a positive state of being. Optimizing your SPIFE will optimize your life!

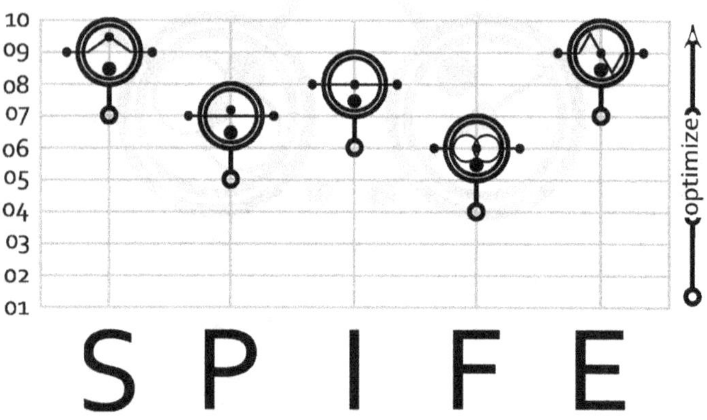

CHAPTER 4: **TRUE-SELF**

Life can be viewed from two perspectives: the outer ego or the inner self. The inner self can also be called the true-self.

Our ego is the outward, self-created portrait of what we want the world to see. It is a facade. It is constantly searching for approval from others and is always in need of being in control. Our ego's perspective or reference point is based in fear. Fear of not fitting in or being liked. Fear of what other people think. Fear of losing influence or power yet, it can be easily influenced or broken. Our ego does not know how to forgive or ask for forgiveness. Because it is based in fear, even the expression of love makes it feel weak or vulnerable. Everything our ego does is concerned with outward appearances. Our ego is always longing, thirsting for some form of outward approval. It is a thirst that will never be quenched.

Our ego will never be satisfied because superficial gain or success is never satisfying. Because of fear, our ego will not acknowledge its weaknesses, failures, or defects and without that acknowledgment, there is no room for change or growth.

I must admit that our ego is a part of who we are, and at times may be necessary in our social dealings. We gain self-esteem and pride through our ego, but if they remain ego based, they will fade. We should avoid living our lives solely based on our ego's perspective. It must be kept under control. Our ego is not who we truly are. Therefore, it would be impossible to access and optimize our SPIFE from an ego's perspective.

Fear is our true enemy.

Fear is bondage that enslaves us from the freedom of truth. Because of fear, we avoid seeking the truth. We are too afraid of what the truth may be. Truth, however, is freedom. Courage is the ability to overcome our fear and seek the truth. Knowing the truth breaks the shackles of fear and sets us free. True freedom is the portal to the pathway of endless possibilities where fear cannot exist. Only our true-self can travel this pathway.

Ultimately our goal is to take on a true-self perspective. True-self is the realization that we are all a part of something much larger than ourselves and we are no greater or no less than anyone else. We have no fear of how we may appear to others. We no longer look outwardly to others for approval, instead we look inwardly to ourselves.

Because our true-self does not need outward

approval from others, we have no fear of failure, loss, or disappointment. We aren't afraid to express anything that may give the appearance of being weak or vulnerable. Our true-self recognizes strength in the expression of love and the ability to ask for forgiveness and to forgive. A true-self perspective allows us to be at peace with who we are and to accept who we are in the present moment. We no longer have to prove our point of view or explain who we are to anyone.

Self-esteem is intrinsic with this perspective. We develop a desire to be better in our own eyes as opposed to the eyes of others. Self-improvement and personal growth happen naturally because of that reason. Our true-self does not live in fear; therefore, we can experience the love, joy, and inner peace that exist where fear cannot. A true-self perspective makes it easy to access and optimize our SPIFE because we are already in tune with it.

Our true-self is our SPIFE!

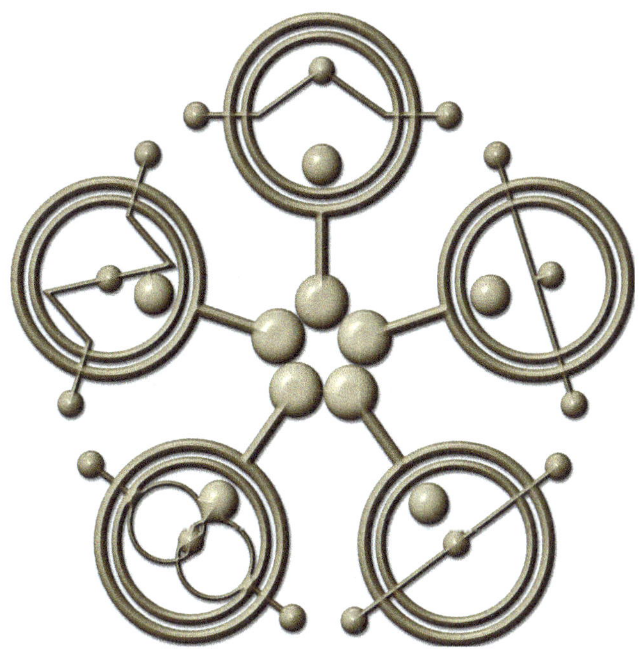

CHAPTER 5: **SPIFE UNAWARE**

Consider your life for a moment. What are some of the things you discuss with the people in your life? They are simple, everyday issues that we don't even think twice about. Here are just a few examples:

- (I) I saw a great documentary about...
- (P) Man, I need to get back into the gym.
- (F) Congrats on your raise!
- (P) I'm finally getting over this cold.
- (E) I have a new boyfriend!
- (E) I just broke up with my girlfriend.
- (F) My rich uncle left me some money.
- (F) My lights got turned off.
- (S) I have a nice book on meditation.
- (P) I road five miles on my bike yesterday.
- (I) I am taking a cooking class.
- (F)When do you start your new job?

- (E) My dad is doing much better.
- (F) I bought a new car.
- (P) How is your diet going?
- (S) Where do you go to pray?
- (E) I like your shoes.
- (I) Try this cool self-improvement book.
- (S) Have you checked your zodiac today?
- (P) I lost twenty pounds!
- (F) I lost twenty dollars!

I can go on and on (some of these examples may fall under several state categories). These are statements and questions that can lead to everyday conversations that take place all over the world every day. Throughout our daily lives, we talk about and are concerned with these things because they affect our lives directly.

We are constantly concerned with all our states, without consciously focusing on them. Some people put more emphasis on their physical states, while others on their spiritual. Some people are mostly interested in their financial state. Whatever the case, at some point, we are all concerned with every state of being to some degree. When life's circumstances shift, our focus on certain states of being also shifts. For example, when we get sick, our physical state becomes our focus or when we have a big test, our intellectual state becomes our focus.

The concept of SPIFE is to acknowledge all our states as being equally important, all the time and to consciously evaluate our states. When we optimize them through exercises and practices, we become more balanced and complete.

CHAPTER 6: **SPIFE HABITS**

Take control of your life! It is impossible to build a house without first having a plan and then implementing that plan. The same is true when building a new life. So... make a plan and do it! I have read it takes from twenty-one to twenty-eight days of doing the same thing to form a habit (good or bad). Forming good habits requires dedication and discipline. It's your life to make it as you desire. You are in complete control.

Dedicate time to optimizing each individual state. I have an early morning routine that covers meditation, reading, journaling, and exercise. It all takes from one to two hours. Give yourself more time to focus on your SPIFE... to focus on yourself. Plan to go to the gym or get some form of exercise for an hour, at least three times a week. Set aside time to meditate or get out into nature. Give yourself time to read something that empowers and inspires you. I recommend beginning your focus on yourself first thing in the morning before you open yourself up to the world. It will reinforce your SPIFE with positive fortitude.

Plan your daily and weekly schedule:

Your daily schedule should be based on your everyday life. It is a good idea to write it down in a planner or save it on your computer. There are multiple daily planner apps available to download to your phone also.

Most of us have a job of some sort, or school that occupies most of our time. Let's refer to those days as our "workday" and our days off, which we'll call our "off day."

Are you an early riser or do you stay up late? Whether you get up at four in the morning or four in the afternoon, the way you begin your day is vital as it sets the tone for the rest of your workday.

When I first wake up, I immediately input positivity and optimism into my mind. I call it my "personal inspirational talk." I take from one to two minutes each morning, before getting out of bed to inspire and motivate myself. I might state a declaration like, "Today, I am in control of my life and my future," or "The only way it will happen is when I make it happen." You know who you are and what is going on in your life. You know what will galvanize you.

Begin your day in control! Try a short meditation first to get your mind aligned with your daily agenda. Schedule at least an hour to prepare for your day before you start your routine of getting ready to leave. Make your breakfast and eat without rushing. Create a routine that allows you to get ready for your day without chaos. When I was a teenager, I used to watch a great TV show called "Get Smart." The good guys were "Control," and the bad guys were "Chaos" (Sorry for the slight digression, but it is so fitting). Starting your day in control will better prepare you for what lies ahead. I always feel like I'm ahead of the day when I begin it in control. Conversely, I feel like I can't keep up when I start my day with chaos.

When planning for your exercise time consider when you have the most energy during your day. Schedule your exercise time around your high energy time for maximum benefit. Try to give yourself one hour for exercise at least three times a week.

Your weekly schedule is a combination of your workday schedule with most of the days being the same, with some slight variations. The off days may be different than your workday. However, it should still include some form of structure that is the same as your workday to stay in practice. For instance, you may want to continue going to bed and getting up at the same time as your workdays. Always add fun, rest, and relaxation to your schedule to allow yourself to get away from your agenda and goals for a little while. Also, make time to reconnect with loved ones to reinforce your esteem and mental support. Be sure to give and receive the love and peace that comes with that connection.

Don't become too attached to your plan, instead remain open to changes that may occur to further enhance it. A plan is fluid, not rigid. Your schedule doesn't have to be stringent, make it somewhat flexible. Give yourself some room for unexpected things. Write it down. Try it, adjust it, and fine-tune it until it works for you.

Most importantly... do it!

Creating routines leads to good habits which are essential when applying SPIFE to your everyday life. Once your habits begin to form, SPIFE optimization becomes natural. You won't have to think everything through, your responses and actions will become instinctive.

"In the present; you have the power to create the future that you want." Tri

CHAPTER 7: **FOCUS**

Focus: [foh-kuhs]

I am going to go on a slight, yet important tangent from the main topic; SPIFE. However, this tangent is a necessary factor in achieving SPIFE optimization, personal growth, and all life accomplishments...

Focus: I have used the word focus numerous times throughout this guide. As I was reading through this guide, I thought this would be the perfect place to expound on what it means to focus.

What is focus?

1. A central point, as of attraction, attention, or activity.

2. Close attention or concentration.

3. The ability to concentrate one's attention or to sustain concentration.

(dictionary.com)

These are the dictionary's definitions of focus. Let's apply that to your life. How does it affect your goals? More specifically, can your goals be achieved without it? You can/will only achieve what you focus on. This is a fundamental truth. For example, if you plan a trip to Chicago, but you focus on Denver. Where will you end up? If you want to be an architect, but you focus on law. What will you become?

Focus is vital! If you have a plan and know what your goal is, the goal must be your focus. Your entire being must be in one accord with one focus. Anything else is a distraction.

Distraction is the adversary of focus!

When you have a goal that you desperately want to achieve, the first step is to rid yourself of all distractions. It is that simple. This includes people and the relationships you have with them. There are some people in your life that are beneficial and others that are detrimental to your goals. The beneficial people will contribute to you achieving your goals. The detrimental people will distract you from your goals. There are other distractions also. A bad or unsatisfying job, an unsupportive living situation, or trying to hold onto something that you can't afford like a house or car. The list of distractions is long and may vary from person to person. First, you must acknowledge your distractions. Secondly, you must learn to accept who or what fits into which category (beneficial or detrimental) and then decide what is most important, the distraction or the goal. This can be a difficult decision, but it is one you must make as the first, most crucial step towards achieving your goal.

Honestly, it is not that simple when it comes to people. We are social beings and form many attachments to many people. Some attachments last for years weather good or bad. It is not easy to detach from those long-time relationships. However, a personal choice must be made. You don't have to completely sever ties, but maybe spend less time with that person. By the way, time away will give each person a chance to heal, which may allow for a possible fresh start or rejuvenation of that relationship later. Consider whether or not you need time apart and choose what is best for you.

With all distractions out of your way, you can completely focus on your goal. To truly achieve your goal, it must become the center of your life. It must become your primary focus. Everything you do should be in line with your goal directly or indirectly. Directly meaning actions such as completing projects, having meetings, taking classes, etc.

Indirectly meaning eating right, exercising, rest and spiritual rejuvenation… you know; SPIFE optimization!

We have just one life on this earth so we should live it completely. We should enjoy each moment. We may have goals that we want to achieve immediately but we should take the time to treasure the journey… the quest… each step of the way. Always focus on the goal but live in every step towards it!

"You can/will only achieve what you focus on." Tri

CHAPTER 8: **SPIFE OPTIMIZATION**

Optimize[op-tuh-mahyz]:

verb(used with object), op·ti·mized, op·ti·miz·ing.

1. to make it as effective, perfect, or useful as possible.

2. to make the best of.

verb(used without object), op·ti·mized, op·ti·miz·ing.

1. to be optimistic.

(dictionary.com)

As I stated earlier, the is no "one way" to optimize your SPIFE. We are all unique individuals and are comprised of many distinct aspects of our being. We do share some similarities also. I must again reiterate the importance of knowing yourself before you can begin to apply SPIFE optimization to your life. Each morning and night you should do a brief assessment of your SPIFE levels. Create a

SPIFE journal. It's a fantastic way to track what affects you and how to better prepare you for similar situations in the future.

SPIFE optimization is accomplished through exercise and practice. Knowing yourself will help you identify where you are weak and what you can use to make yourself stronger, where you are lacking and what you can do to improve. Each state of being can use specific exercises and practices for the enhancement of that state. Because of their synergistic relationship, each state of being is influenced (positively or negatively) by the other, improving one will help to improve the other. Some exercises can perform multiple enhancements by affecting multiple states at the same time.

The terms "exercise" and "practice" go together like hand in glove. You can practice an exercise or exercise a practice. A couple of examples are: When you go to the gym, you can practice your exercise of lifting weights properly. At home, you can exercise your practice of meditation. In the following chapters, I will explore the various types of exercises and practices that can optimize each state of being.

You might be thinking, " Man, can't I take a break from this SPIFE stuff for a while?" That is like saying, "Man, can't I take a break from my life for a while?" SPIFE is your life. The better your SPIFE, the better your life!

Optimizing your SPIFE will create an outward energy of positivity. The perception that you generate will produce an exact perception of you. The way you are perceived is how people will respond to you (positively or negatively). This is from a true-self perspective, not ego.

CHAPTER 9: **SPIFE SYMBOLS**

I am an artist and a very visual person. So, I created five symbols to represent the five states of our SPIFE. Below is a diagram that describes the meaning of each aspect of the state of being symbol...

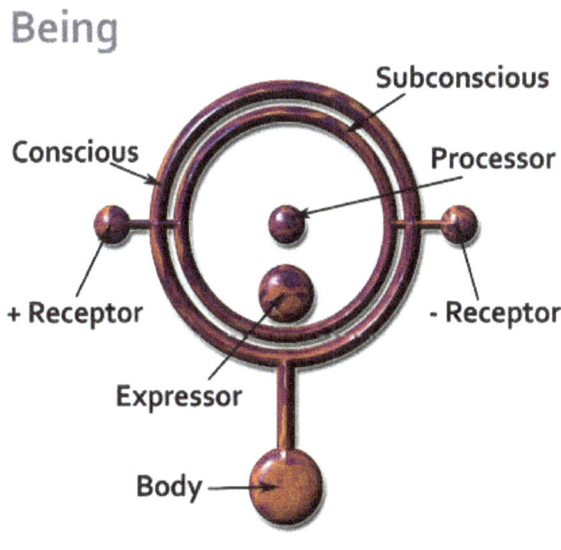

SPIFE Symbol Descriptors

The state of being symbols are a fun way to visualize each state. Every day we are bombarded with positive and negative things that affect us and our SPIFE as a whole and each state individually. We have positive and negative receptors that take in the information through our senses (sight, hearing, smell, etc.). The information goes to our processor (brain). As we process the information, it begins to affect our conscious and subconscious minds which in turn molds and shapes us into who we are. Through our expressor, we show the world who we are in a variety of ways such as through music, art, poetry, teaching, etc.

CHAPTER 10: **SPIRITUAL STATE**

SPIRITUAL OPTIMIZATION:

What is spiritual? It has been said that we are not bodies that have a soul, but souls that have a body. The descriptions may vary depending on points of view. So, here is my point of view. It is a personal experience. Spiritual or spirituality is the belief in something beyond the scientific description of physical existence. The acknowledgment that all living things are a part of something much greater than ourselves. It is a connection to the universe and the universal flow of energy that exist in everything. It is not religion; however, it is possible to be obtained through religion. It could be the belief in a god or gods, the universe or nature. Whatever the case, it offers something to draw strength from... to plug into for rejuvenation. No matter what your spiritual beliefs may be, the concept of SPIFE can still apply to you and your life.

There are several ways to optimize our spiritual state. Here are a few examples:

• Meditate: Meditation is an excellent way to settle your mind to plug into the Universal energy that connects and surrounds everything. Practice meditating as often as possible to develop a deeper and more enriched meditation experience.

• Prayer: Much like meditation, prayer is a way to connect with something greater than yourself. Whatever your belief may be, the practice of prayer will strengthen your spiritual connection.

• Nature: Getting out of the city and back into nature for some time can do wonders for your spiritual state. It offers you a chance to get away from your problems and focus on what really matters... the joy of just being alive. While in nature, try meditation or prayer to further enhance your experience.

- Read: There are many books out there that can help or guide you in your spiritual experience. If you know yourself, you will know what works for you.

My Personal Spiritual State of Being:

What Affects My Spiritual State?

How can I optimize my Spiritual State?

How can I use my other states to optimize my Spiritual State?

CHAPTER 11: **PHYSICAL STATE**

PHYSICAL OPTIMIZATION:

Our body is our physical home. It is our connection to the physical world and the physical universe. We use it to receive information and as a tool for expression. Without our physical body, we cannot exist on this physical plane. We must take great care of it because it is the only one we've got.

There are several ways to optimize our physical state. Here are a few examples:

• Nourishment: They say you are what you eat. Whether you are an omnivore, vegetarian or vegan. What you put into your body will have a lasting effect on it. Maintaining a healthy diet is a key factor in staying physically fit. This includes plenty of fresh, clean, and pure water. I also recommend adding natural vitamin supplements to your diet.

• Rest: This part of our physical state is often overlooked or taken for granted. Rest is arguably the most important aspect of physical optimization. Rest helps us heal and rejuvenate. It is recommended that an adult gets seven to nine hours of sleep every day. You know yourself; you know what the best rest time for you is.

- Exercise: Our bodies are biological machines and require activity to remain strong. Its response is simple; you exercise it you get stronger; you don't you get weaker. The resistance created through lifting weights challenges your muscles and bones and in turn, makes them stronger. Simply taking a brisk walk daily for at least thirty minutes will improve your physical state. Join a gym or get a personal trainer. Buy your own gym equipment for your home. If you live in an apartment complex that has a gym, use it. There are free apps that offer excellent exercise programs that can be done in the comfort of your home. Make exercise a part of your daily routine.

My Personal Physical State of Being:

What Affects My Physical State?

How can I optimize my Physical State?

How can I use my other states to optimize my Physical State?

CHAPTER 12: **INTELLECTUAL STATE**

INTELLECTUAL OPTIMIZATION:

Our intellectual state of being... our mind. We experience things – positive or negative - through our senses (sight, hearing, smell, taste, touch) and process the information in our minds. We are in complete control of our lives because everything that happens to us takes place in our minds. How we choose to respond to any situation or circumstance solely affects how we live our lives every moment. How we choose is determined by our state of mind.

There are several ways to optimize our intellectual state. Here are a few examples:

- Study: Add new knowledge through books, documentaries, and classes/teachings. Take a class online or at your local college. If there is something you want to know, learn it. These are excellent ways to grow your intellect.

- Conversation: Try talking to someone who doesn't always share the same point of view to challenge your intellect. Your mind is not much different than your body. Just like the resistance created through lifting weights challenges your muscles and bones and in turn, makes them stronger. The same is true for your mind. Challenging thoughts and ideas can serve to strengthen your mind. Therefore, daily mind exercise should be practiced.

- Rest: Physical rest is vital in maintaining an optimal intellectual state. While our conscious rest it allows our subconscious time to process what we have received throughout the day.

- Meditation: Meditation is another way to quiet our conscious to allow our subconscious to process our thoughts.

- Read: Reading can have several effects on our intellect. Reading sparks the imagination and helps us open our minds to infinite possibilities.

My Personal Intellectual State of Being:

What Affects My Intellectual State?

How can I optimize my Intellectual State?

How can I use my other states to optimize my Intellectual State?

CHAPTER 13: **FINANCIAL STATE**

FINANCIAL OPTIMIZATION:

My view of our financial state is more than the sole focus on money. However, avoid anyone who tells you money is bad or evil. It is not. Money is an immensely powerful tool that can be used for good or bad. It can aid in any endeavor and frankly, can make your life better. Don't be afraid to attain money. It's been said, "The only people who don't care about money are the people who don't have it."

Money is extremely important in our lives, however our financial state of being is comprised of other factors as well. How do you interact with others to reach a mutual agreement? Are you charismatic? Do you pursue a "win-win" scenario in your business dealings?

There are several ways to optimize our financial state. Here are a few examples:

• Study: If you have a particular career in mind, you will have to learn everything about it. Go to a university or local college. Go to trade school. Get a job in the field which you would like to pursue. Start at the bottom, work your way up and learn everything you possibly can along the way.

• Read: Study books on finance from saving to investing. Learn from someone who has already been where you are trying to go. Read self-growth and self-improvement books to help you create the proper mindset to achieve your financial goals.

- Plan: Make a plan. Write it down in your planner and put it on your computer and phone for easy reference. Remember, don't become too attached to your plan, instead remain open to changes that may occur to further enhance it.

- Implement: Just do it! Don't procrastinate or hesitate. The only way to achieve success is to start towards it. Each step is an accomplishment that can inspire and motivate you to take the next step. Keep your focus on your goal but approach it one step at a time.

My Personal Financial State of Being:

What Affects My Financial State?

How can I optimize my Financial State?

How can I use my other states to optimize my Financial State?

CHAPTER 14: **EMOTIONAL STATE**

EMOTIONAL OPTIMIZATION:

When I think about people (myself included), I sometimes think that we are entirely comprised of emotions alone. It does seem to be the driving force behind everything we do. There is always the constant battle of controlling our emotions. However, further review proves that we are much more than that. The emotional state does seem to require more attention and effort for optimization. The effect it has on the other states is tremendous, but likewise, the effects of the other states on it are equally substantial. This is recognized and completely accepted in the philosophy of SPIFE. SPIFE says to embrace all of your emotions for they play a key role in what makes us human. Learn to understand why you feel what you feel and use your SPIFE to help create balance within your emotions.

There are several ways to optimize your emotional state. Here are a few examples:

• Meditate: Meditation is a wonderful way to settle your mind to tap into the Universal energy. Through meditation you can quiet your mind to allow peaceful thoughts to enter.

• Prayer: Much like meditation, prayer is a way to connect with something greater than yourself. Whatever your belief may be, the practice of prayer will strengthen your spiritual connection.

• Read: Find books that are uplifting and inspirational. Whether you enjoy science fiction or romance novels, try a book that takes you away from the worries of everyday life.

• Express: Talk to a friend or loved one. Recording your thoughts with a recording app or journal. If necessary, get professional help. There is no shame in asking for help.

- Nature: Getting out of the city and back into nature for a while can do wonders for your emotional state also. As stated earlier, it offers you a chance to get away from your problems and focus on what really matters... the joy of just being alive. Spend time in nature as often as possible. Take in the fresh air and the wonderfully peaceful sounds of nature. Get back in touch with that natural person within you.

- Non-judgment: Let things be as they are. Over-analyzing and over-thinking can cause turbulence in your mind. Settle your mind by accepting things as they are, not how you want them to be. Avoid trying to foresee or anticipate the future. Live in the present moment.

My Personal Emotional State of Being

What Affects My Emotional State?

How can I optimize my Emotional State?

How can I use my other states to optimize my Emotional State?

Chapter 15: **SPIFE SUMMARY**

SPIFE optimization, along with a true-self perspective is the key to living a better, more complete life. Knowing yourself will improve your ability to optimize each state through specific exercises and practices. Developing a daily and weekly routine to create good SPIFE habits will cause an instinctual SPIFE reaction to any situation or circumstance. When you change your focus away from your problems and onto yourself, you begin to view your problems as challenges and the challenges become new opportunities for learning and growth. Being aware of the synergistic power of your states will equip you with the tools you need to take control of your life in the driver's seat of your life's quest.

PART 2: **SPIFE** BUBBLE

CHAPTER 1: **YOUR WORLD**

Imagine your world as a bubble of which the center of that bubble is... you! You are the sole controller, unequivocal ruler, creator, and destroyer. You are the sun, the moon, and the stars. You cause the weather to change at will, with a simple thought. Sadness and sorrow can exist in your bubble, but happiness and joy can as well. You have the power to make your world - your bubble – into any type of place you want and can change it any time you want! This is your space where you reside. It is your home, your haven in which you are its life source. It is where you go to rest and rejuvenate. When you need to escape from the turmoil of the world, your bubble is your refuge.

New thoughts and ideas are realized within your bubble. Your bubble is you and your SPIFE is its main influencer.

You are always in your SPIFE bubble, no matter where you are or where you go. The size of your bubble may fluctuate depending on your state of mind, mood or situation. It may expand to allow room for others to enter or compress for only you to fit. One moment it can be transparent and bright, the next, clouded and dark. Sometimes it can be rigid and impenetrable, other times, flexible and open. Whatever your state may be will determine the state of your bubble.

Since your bubble is your world that only you reside in, how do you want it to be? Remember, you have complete control of every aspect of your world. Do you want a world of peace or turmoil? Do you want joy or sorrow? The choice is entirely yours.

You have the ability to let whatever is happening outside your world in or keep it out. If you want peace, love, and happiness in your world, use your SPIFE to create it.

The atmosphere of your bubble can change with a simple thought. You can cause the sun to shine or the rain to fall despite what is happening outside. The outside world could be caught in a raging storm while inside your bubble is a tranquil paradise. It is what you make it! The things we experience in life only affect us the way we allow them to, and we have a choice of how... every time. What we choose directly affects our bubble and makes our world the way it is at that moment. Using your SPIFE combined with a true-self perspective, you can create a bubble of peace, joy, and happiness where the sun is always shining.

CHAPTER 2: **WORLD CENTER**

You are the center of your world. What happens to your bubble if you try to make someone else the center of your world?

We do it all the time. We fall in love and become infatuated with a person so much that we begin to live for them. They become the center of our world. Whether it is a friend, a romantic love, a spouse, or even a parent or child. Our feelings for them can sometimes lead to them becoming the main focus of our life. Situations and circumstances may force us to feel as though we must make them the center of our world. For example, when someone gets extremely ill or terribly injured, and we take on the responsibility of caring for them. New love or love that is ending (and everything in between) can cause us to make someone the center of our world. They begin to rule our thoughts and consume our lives. After a while, we start to lose focus on the most important person in our bubble... ourselves.

The main problem with making someone the center of your bubble is... it's your bubble! Two people cannot occupy one world or one bubble at the same time. You are meant to be the center, the main focus of your world at all times. They are never truly the center of your bubble; it just appears so because you allow them to be. This creates a false world, a false reality that can lead to chaos and madness.

They become your sunshine and rain, your happiness and sadness depending on their mood or state of being. You begin to lose control of your world and become subject to their wishes and desires. If they are happy - your world is happy. If they are sad - your world is sad. When you rely on someone else for the happiness, joy, and peace they may bring when they enter your world, you no longer find those emotions on your own. You surrender the ability to create those emotions for yourself, within your bubble. Because of that, you only experience them when that person is around, but when that person leaves, the happiness, joy, and peace leave with them. You are left alone in your bubble without control. You cannot make the sunshine anymore.

We are social beings and personal relationships are vital to our survival individually and as a species. A healthy, happy relationship involves... requires healthy, happy individuals. Each must be whole or complete within themselves already. One should not need the other to become whole, complete, or... happy. The problems always arise when one begins to rely on another for what is lacking within themself. They start to surrender control of their own world right at that moment. This can cause turmoil in any type of relationship. Pressure and stress begins to build within each individual for various reasons.

For one, it is the feeling of being responsible for someone else's emotions while maintaining their own. Because of this, they focus on the person who is lacking by trying to make up for what is missing. They lose focus on themselves. They begin to make the other person the center of their bubble.

For the other, it is the reliance on someone else for their emotional stability. This is ironic because what it creates is less stability in both bubbles. They focus on the other person for all of their emotional needs. They begin to make the other person the center of their bubble.

The result of the relationship is two people

people who have lost focus on themselves and are no longer the center of their own bubbles. They become codependent on each other in a false reality. This can go on for years but, eventually it will fall apart. This situation cannot...will not last, because it is impossible to be the center of someone else's world. One can only be the center of their own world... their own bubble.

The balance in the relationship is lost and the struggle to regain that balance starts to affect the relationship. There comes a time when one or the other recognizes the need to be the center of their own bubble once again. They begin to focus on themselves, which is immediately apparent to the other person. As they move back to being the center of their own world, the other begins to feel lost and afraid. They see the other as selfish and unconcerned. They begin to feel abandoned and unloved. The false center of their world is leaving, and they don't know what to do...

The answer is simple, they too must regain control of their own world. They must use their SPIFE to help them focus on becoming the center of their bubble. They need to become complete within their own world.

Once both are back in control of their own worlds at the center of their own bubbles, the healing process can begin. There is now hope for their relationship. Two complete people working together, begin to view their problems as challenges and opportunities for growth. They can then use the growth to strengthen their relationship.

Although they appear to be the same, there can be a slight difference between selfish and self-centered. In this case, you can be self-centered without being selfish. You should always be the center of your bubble. You can do so and still be concerned with the well-being of others. You can still show love and kindness. When you are the center of your world, and your world is at peace you can become selfless without the risk of losing control of your bubble.

You may sometimes get lost in a relationship by making the other person the center of your bubble. When you feel yourself surrendering control of your world, the first thing you must do is regain control of your bubble. Do what it takes to become the center of your world once again. Get back to the root and core of who you are.

Get back to your SPIFE. Use your SPIFE to take charge of your world... your life! Focus on your SPIFE and in turn, focus on yourself and your bubble. Re-establish yourself as the sole controller, unequivocal ruler, creator, and destroyer of your world once again! Once you are back in control of your bubble, use your SPIFE to rebuild and recreate the world that you want for yourself. Re-establish your bubble as your haven and safe place of peace and love.

Make your sun shine again or, make it rain. It's your choice... it's your world.

Promise yourself to never allow anyone – no matter who it is – to take control of your world... your bubble, ever again!

CHAPTER 3: **OTHER WORLDS**

Everyone lives within their own bubble. One of the problems we may face is being concerned with someone else and what is going on in their world... their bubble. We begin to speculate and create our scenarios about what we think could be happening in their world. Trying to figure out what is happening in someone else's bubble is like living on Earth yet, trying to know what is happening on Mars.

I was laying in my bed early one morning, contemplating what was happening in someone else's life. I hadn't seen nor talked to this person in a while and yet there I was, trying to somehow figure out their life. I found myself creating baseless scenarios that I would play over in my mind. Anxiety and frustration began to build as I fell deeper into my self-created story of their world. I got so deep into this false reality; my mind began to accept it as real. The sadness, anger, and frustration became real. The anxiety became real. I needed some resolve for the imaginary situation I created. Unfortunately, I continued my resolve still based on my unfounded scenario. I created solutions based on my imagination. This all saturated my mind so much that I began to resent the person.

Of course, the truth was, the possibilities of what was really happening in their bubble were endless. As it later turned out, I was completely wrong about everything I was thinking. All of the things I had imagined didn't come close to the reality of what was actually happening in their life. Even more, if I really wanted to know what was happening in their life, I should have just asked them. I could have saved myself from wasted energy, anxiety, and stress, had I simply focused on my own bubble. I know this sounds silly but, "Stay in your bubble, stay out of trouble."

CHAPTER 4: **WORLDS COLLIDE**

The atmosphere of our bubble can also be recognized as our aura or vibe. As we live our lives and go about our daily activities, we encounter one another in many different ways, constantly entering and exiting each other's bubbles. We may sometimes encounter someone who has an atmosphere that is so strong that we can almost feel what is happening in their bubble without actually interacting with them. This can be a positive or negative experience.

I find it to be remarkably interesting that even in a crowded place like a mall or busy sidewalk, most of the time, no interaction takes place. We seem to avoid interacting with one another. Maybe it's because of fear. Fear of the unknown or fear of our own inadequacies. Sometimes there is interaction. A simple hello or good morning creates some form of interaction or connection. The longer the interaction, the more time spent intermingling bubbles. While intermingling, we begin to learn about each other and see what it is like in the other's bubble. One bubble begins to affect and influence the other. Eventually, the connection ends, and each person goes their separate ways. However, there is still a residual effect on each individual's bubble. It can dissipate immediately or linger for a while, depending on the connection.

Some interactions can be amazing while others may be downright miserable. Sometimes a real connection is made, and you don't want it to end. The experience shared when two bubbles intermingle in a positive way can be so enjoyable that it becomes difficult when it is time to part. The atmosphere of each bubble and the intermingling of them can create a space of love, joy and peace that can be almost overwhelming. We sometimes long for reconnection. We make it possible to reconnect again by exchanging personal information and reconnect as soon as possible.

How would you affect someone's bubble? Would they want to interact with you again? Is your bubble a place where the atmosphere is noticeable from a distance? Ponder these questions while at work or while attending a large event with a lot of other bubbles present. Think about it as your bubble enters and exits other bubbles. Consider the affect they have on you and the affect you have on them. What impression or residual effect do you want to leave the people you come into contact with?

CHAPTER 5: **BUBBLE SUMMARY**

Your bubble is your own personal world. You have the power to make your world anyway you want it to be and can change it anytime you want. It can be a place of peace and happiness or of turmoil and sadness. It is completely up to you. Use your SPIFE to create the world that you want. Your bubble is your haven and refuge. Remember, only you can be the center of your world and you must do what it takes to always remain its center. Focus on your bubble and avoid contemplating someone else's bubble. Your bubble is your world and with your SPIFE at optimal levels, your bubble will have an optimistically optimized atmosphere!

A simple observation...

Most people are good people. They stay in their bubble because that is where they feel safe from the outside world. They are afraid to let other people enter their bubbles. I am very outgoing and am not afraid to speak to strangers. I have noticed that people I see, sometimes daily, will not speak or even look at me as we pass each other. They appear to be none social or introverted. People want... need to connect, but the fear of – who knows what (you can fill in the blank) – inhibits their connecting. Then, one day I decided to simply say, "hello" to them and I discovered a person that is completely different than I expected. Try that sometime... say hello to someone and you will be surprised by the response you get!

PART 3: **EMBRACE YOUR QUEST**

"Our purpose... our reason for existing in simple. We want to help you transition from helplessness to helpfulness!" EYQ

CHAPTER 1: **INTRODUCTION**

Embrace Your Quest

I said this way back on page seven of this guide:

"As you travel through life - taking what life gives you and going where life leads you - your life is a journey. The journey ends when you decide to take charge of your life and to live it on your terms... your life becomes a quest!"

Everything (that takes place after your journey becomes your quest) is ALL a part of your quest. You have a goal that you are striving to achieve. Along the way you experience obstacles and challenges that seem to distract, divert or delay your progress towards your goal. Those things are a part of your quest. They are placed in your pathway to evaluate and teach you... to prepare you for what is coming next. Everything you experience is connected to your quest. When you encounter these challenges, you must accept them as a part of your quest and therefor embrace them… you must embrace your quest!

The concept of "Embrace Your Quest or EYQ", actually came before SPIFE. After I discovered my purpose, I began working on ways to help better my life with hopes to eventually help others better their lives. My first thought was, "What has and would help me?" I began to formulate ways to take charge of my life. My first thoughts were decision making. We all have choices to make daily and those choice decisions affect our lives in the present and in the future. As I pondered my past choices, I realized one common truth. In most cases the decisions weren't necessarily good or bad, but more of a directional effect. By that I mean that the decisions changed the direction my life was heading in. They either kept me headed in the same direction or changed my direction slightly or greatly. In terms or goal setting and focus, did the decisions help or hurt my pursuit? I wanted to keep it simple by suggesting that all decisions are either beneficial or detrimental to the direction of our pathway and the pursuance of our goals.

SPIFE came about because I realized that I needed to change within myself to pursue my goals in an optimum state of being.

I knew I needed to be more organized with a plan. I created a process that would break down the steps towards achieving a goal. The world of EYQ is vast. This is just a summary of what EYQ is about.

CHAPTER 2: **TERMINOLOGIES**

I created a table of terms to establish a common language and since of structure within EYQ. My goal was and still is to help people move their ideas from the idea (almost spiritual) realm - through the portal of a plan - and into the physical realm by creating a realistic plan that can be easily implemented. What is a plan that is never implemented? It is an idea that only exist in one's mind. To have a plan that works, one must first know how to create a plan. The table below are the terms that I have chosen to use when developing a plan.

The plan may consist of many steps, stages, and phases to achieve a goal. A mission may consist of several goals and a vision may consist of several missions. A vision is the ultimate goal because through it is how your true purpose is attained.

Embrace Your Quest Table of Terminologies

Quest　　　**D:** A self-guided journey with an intentional goal

Beneficial　　**D:** A decision that is positive; towards a quest goal

Decision　　**R:** The decision was beneficial; The decision was detrimental

Detrimental　**D:** A decision that is negative; against a quest goal

Purpose　　**D:** Your life's ambition; The reason for which you exist

Perceive　　**R:** To perceive a purpose; A purpose is perceived

Attain　　　**R:** To attain a purpose; A purpose is attained

Vision　　　**D:** The culmination of all missions and goals; your true purpose

Realize　　**R:** To realize a vision; A vision is realized

Mission　　**D:** The more adamant goal; consist of many goals towards one outcome

Accomplish	**R:** To accomplish a mission; A mission is accomplished
Goal	**D:** The focus of a plan; an idea made physical
Achieve	**R:** To achieve a goal; A goal is achieved
Plan	**D:** The doorway/portal between the idea realm and the physical realm.
Conceive	**R:** To conceive a plan; A plan is conceived
Phase	**D:** A sub-goal within a plan
Complete	**R:** To complete a phase; A phase is completed
Stage	**D:** A sub-goal within a phase
Set	**R:** To set a stage; A stage is set
Step	**D:** The physical action towards a goal
Take	**R:** To take a step; A step is taken
Idea	**D:** The moment a dream begins to materialize
Own	**R:** To own an idea; An idea is owned

Dream	**D:** The spiritual vision. A desire that wants to be realized

Realize	**R:** To realize a dream; A dream is realized

D: The EYQ definition of the term.   R: The EYQ relationship to the term.

Study the words with thier definitions.Notice the corresponding words and the relationship they have with each other. The entire process is the complete embodiment of your true purpose!

Embrace Your Quest will take form as an interactive website/blog based community created to help individuals transition from helplessness to helpfulness!

ENJOY THE MOMENT...

With each idea... enjoy the moment
Live in every idea

With each plan... enjoy the moment
Live in every plan

With each step... enjoy the moment
Live in every step

With each challenge... enjoy the moment
Live in every challenge

With each achievement... enjoy the moment
Live in every achievement

With each gift... enjoy the moment
Live in every gift

With each gratitude... enjoy the moment
Live in every gratitude

With each celebration... enjoy the moment
Live in every celebration

With each service... enjoy the moment
Live in every service

... Live in the Moment

MY PERSONAL MANTRA

Whatever I do...

I will enjoy the moment

I will give my all - 100% of myself

I will strive for love, peace and happiness

I will cultivate an ''everyone can win" environment

I will think positive-empowering thoughts

I will completely focus on my goals

I will persevere through all adversity

I will persist until the goal is achieved

I will give thanks for my many blessings

I will appreciate and celebrate all my success

I will live free of all constraints

I will help others to succeed

MY PERSONAL NOTE

The world is vast with billions of people who each have their unique view of it. I never thought of myself as a writer (after reading this, some will probably agree with that thought). As I was writing this (actually, this thought occurred to me while making my morning tea), I began to realize that I enjoy writing and concluded that I do want to be a writer. The irony of it all is that I was terrible in English (still the same thought of others who have read this). So much so that if I got a "C" in the class my parents would be satisfied with the grade, as was I. It's not that I didn't work at it. I just didn't get it. For instance: How is it that the words "read and read" are both past and present tense based on the pronunciations? Secondly, why are you able to pronounce them differently when they are spelled the same?! Not to mention the word "red." Then there's "tear and tear" two totally different meanings, and "live and live," two slightly different meanings. Oh, which reminds me, "two, to, and too"(not so bad, at least they are spelled differently). "Grey and gray," can someone please decide? How about this one, "She rode down the road.," and "I can't decide whether or not I like the weather." Here's another one, "I lost my sense of taste since I ate that hot pepper." What the f@$#! I mean it goes on and on! I know I'm not the only one who feels this way because I have had several, different discussions with several, different people on the subject and they completely agree with me. I truly feel for someone who is new to English. I was and am very good at math. I get math. Math makes sense. The English language is awesome but why in the... I'm sorry for the ranting digression. Back to my point. I consider myself an artist first. For me, painting, drawing, and sculpting are my best forms of expression. I've done those things my entire life.

What is an expression? It is a way to show the world who you are, how you see the world, and where you fit into it. Your expression is exclusively yours alone. The more I write, the more I feel the power of expression through it. I am beginning to fall in love with it! I have always had an underlying desire to share my uniquely personal view of the world with the world. I am happy to say that I have found an additional means to do so!

DEDICATIONS

Time for the tears...

I must first express how grateful I am for my family and the love they give me and show me! I dedicate this guide to them. First my mother, Bobbie J. (Fuller) Boyer, who has always been my greatest confidant. My father, Roosevelt A. Boyer Jr. (who is now on his new journey/quest on another plane), for setting the foundation of molding me into the man I am today. My sister Charlia R. Boyer, who has always been my "Jiminy Cricket" and best friend. My cousin Warren D. Hunt, we shared the crib together as babies... my brother. My ex-wife, Eddren A. (Aldridge) Boyer, who is still a vital part of my life. My daughters: Alexandria (Alley), Britainn (Btan), Ravynn (Ravynn-Bavynn), Taleah (Beauty), Jordyn-Nia (Jordy-Pordy - who is actually my niece), and Troi-Madisynn (Little). "Right-on chicks!" I would have to write an entire book to explain the joy, happiness and gratitude I have to the universe for blessing me with you wonderful, beautiful and unique young women in my life. I love you all with all of my being! To my grandkids: Braylon, Rayden, Corinne, and the "Bun in the Oven" girl or boy, the continuing joys of my life!

These are the people I live for each day. They are my "WHY?" They are my main influence and motivation!

BOOK OF SPIFE MISSION

The sole mission of this guide is to somehow help make the world a better place. If SPIFE can help… so be it…

SPIFE up *your life!*

ISBN 979-8-21-073270-5

Published in the United States of America

First Published, 2023

Roosevelt A. Boyer III

www.SPIFE.org

www.ingramcontent.com/pod-product-compliance
Lightning Source LLC
Chambersburg PA
CBHW071200130726

47998CB00002B/552